Gorillas

by Grace Hansen

abdopublishing.com

Published by Abdo Kids, a division of ABDO, PO Box 398166, Minneapolis, Minnesota 55439.

Printed in the United States of America, North Mankato, Minnesota.

052015

092015

 THIS BOOK CONTAINS
RECYCLED MATERIALS

Photo Credits: Corbis, Glow Images, iStock, Science Source, Shutterstock
Production Contributors: Teddy Borth, Jennie Forsberg, Grace Hansen
Design Contributors: Laura Rask, Dorothy Toth

Library of Congress Control Number: 2014958553
Cataloging-in-Publication Data
Hansen, Grace.
 Gorillas / Grace Hansen.
  p. cm. -- (Animal friends)
ISBN 978-1-62970-894-2
Includes index.
1. Gorilla--Juvenile literature.   I. Title.
599.884--dc23
                  2014958553

Table of Contents

Gorillas

Gorillas live in parts of Africa.

They live in forests.

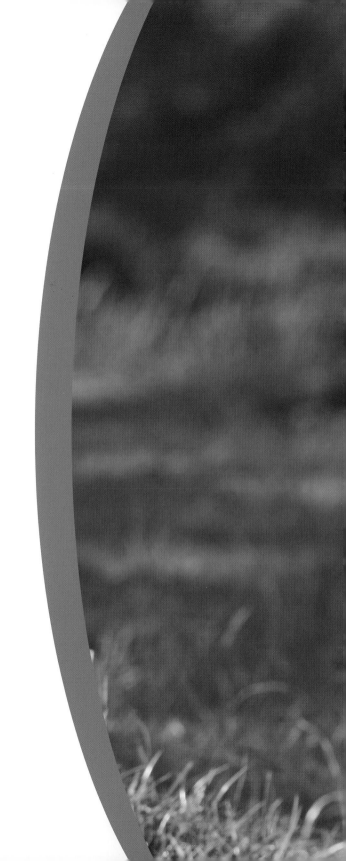

4

Gorillas have brownish hair.

It covers most of their bodies.

6

Gorillas have long arms. Their legs are shorter than their arms. They use all four **limbs** to walk.

9

Food

Gorillas eat flowers and fruits. They also eat leaves and other plant parts. Some eat bugs. They **rarely** eat small animals.

Life in a Band

Gorillas live in groups called **bands**. Each band has about seven gorillas. There is one male and many females and babies.

Protecting Each Other

Poachers set traps to catch gorillas. It is **illegal**. Traps kill many gorillas.

Some gorillas have learned to destroy traps. Older gorillas teach the younger ones.

It would be easy to avoid the traps. But gorillas know that the traps will hurt others.

18

19

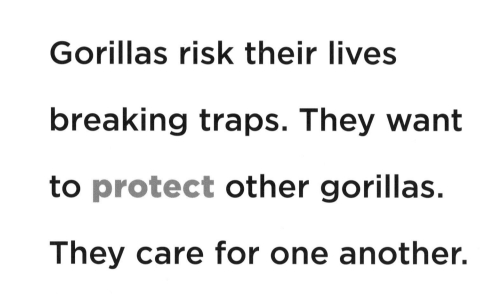

Gorillas risk their lives breaking traps. They want to **protect** other gorillas. They care for one another.

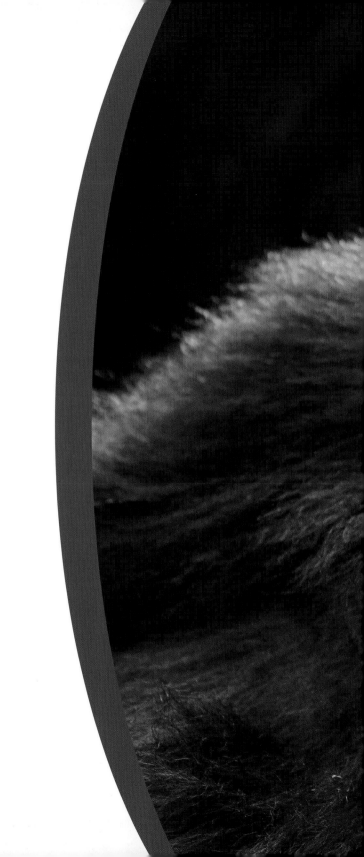

More Facts

- The oldest and largest male gorilla leads the band. He is called a silverback. This is because he has silver hair on his back.

- Gorillas are very powerful. But they are also gentle and shy.

- Gorillas laugh, hug, and play with each other when they are happy.

Glossary

band – a group of gorillas that includes one male and many females and babies.

illegal – against the law.

limb – a leg or arm of a human or an animal.

poacher – one who illegally kills or takes wild animals.

protect – to keep safe from harm.

rarely – not usually.

Index

abdokids.com

Use this code to log on to abdokids.com and access crafts, games, videos, and more!

Abdo Kids Code:
AGK8942